Integration for Adults
with Learning Difficulties

Contexts and Debates

Jeannie Sutcliffe

The National Institute of Adult Continuing Education

First published in 1992 by the National Institute of Adult
Continuing Education (England and Wales)
19B De Montfort Street
Leicester LE1 7GE

Reprinted 1994

British Library Cataloguing-in-Publication Data
A catalogue record for this book is available from the British Library.
ISBN 1 872941 18 4

*Cover design by Paul Vann
Filmset by The Midlands Book Typesetting Company, Loughborough
Printed and bound in Great Britain by
Biddles Ltd, Guildford and King's Lynn*

*Photographs: pages 4, 8, 50, B. Madoc, pages 64 and 70, V. Hallam,
taken during the NIACE/Lancaster University Summer School, August
1991; pages 18, 40 and 90, the Dorset Linking Scheme, Esther James;
page 30, a City and Guilds cookery course at Frome College, Somerset;
page 58, a cookery group at Barking College of Adult Education,
Essex; pages 82 and 100, Gillygate Wholefoods Bakery in York
which offers employment to people with learning difficulties, Raissa
Page/FORMAT.*

Contents

Introduction

The integration, or inclusion, of adults with learning difficulties in adult, further and higher education is an area of work that is slowly developing. This practitioner guide aims to bring together information and ideas from some of the innovative schemes that are offering integrated learning in England and Wales.

Examples of integrated learning in a wide range of contexts are documented, from adult education evening classes to vocational courses at colleges and a university summer school. The case studies reflect the successes and the difficulties in planning for integration. A number of the schemes involve close liaison between education departments, health authorities, social services departments and voluntary organisations. In some cases, the lead agency is either the health authority or the social services department, rather than the education department. Consideration is given to the support needed in terms of backing from managers and policy makers. Issues relating to the participation of people with profound and multiple learning difficulties or challenging behaviour are also highlighted. The final section addresses strategies and incorporates checklists which practitioners and managers will find useful in planning developments. This publication is the first in a series of short, practitioner-oriented books arising from NIACE's development project on adults with learning difficulties. It follows on from the chapter on integration published in the handbook *Adults with Learning Difficulties: Education for choice and empowerment* (Sutcliffe, 1990).

The NIACE project on continuing education for adults with learning difficulties has set out to document good practice in learning opportunities across agencies. Integration was highlighted as an area of particular interest by practitioners on the project network, many of whom are working towards developments in their local areas. This practitioner guide aims to:

- outline some of the debates about integrated learning
- provide examples of integration in action drawn from a range of settings in continuing education

- encourage practitioners to reflect on possible developments in their own area.

The development work for this publication was made possible by funding from the Joseph Rowntree Foundation, the local authorities' associations and from the Department of Education and Science.

Exclusion leads to 'isolation, segregation, loneliness, stigmatisation, oppression and exploitation.'

Inclusion leads to 'community acceptance, being welcomed, being known by one's name instead of being given a label.' (Barbara Lynch, *A Parent's Experience.*)

'Segregation is an erosion of basic human rights. Segregation is an exclusion, a devaluation, discriminating.' (Centre for Studies on Integration in Education.)

Chapter 1

Debates in Integration

People talk of protecting and safeguarding educational provision for adults with learning difficulties. The reality of much existing provision is that 'special' groups have been set up to meet the perceived 'special needs' of adults with learning difficulties. Segregated groups have been the norm, reinforcing the practice of special schools, which isolate and thus make people with learning difficulties seem 'different' and 'apart' from society. A parent has voiced the concern: 'We believe "special" is not always what it may seem to be, but can be a very negative road to travel down' (Forrest, 1991).

> *Integration in education is a moral issue: it is also a human rights issue. And the discussion is therefore about how society views disability or learning difficulties – that is, whether or not it accepts the normality of disability.* (Mark Vaughan, Centre for Studies on Integration in Education.)

There is a growing acceptance that adults with learning difficulties have the right to continue their education after school. This is backed up by the wording of the 1988 Education Reform Act, which informs local education authorities of their responsibility to 'have regard' to the needs of this group of actual and potential students. The full impact of the 1992 Further and Higher Education Act has yet to emerge.

An HMI report notes that: 'Few students with special needs join mainstream courses but more could do so if provided with appropriate support and guidance' (DES/HMI, 1989). Often separate, special groups within adult and further education have developed a limited curriculum centred almost exclusively around skills for independence. Chances to mix and learn with other adults are minimal in these circumstances. As Joe Whittaker has observed:

> *Discrete groups do not lead to a re-launch into the mainstream of college life, but provide the student with another systematic route to further segregated education, which invariably means limited curriculum and restricted progress. Students are being manoeuvred to yet another educational cul-de-sac. The further education system is in the process of establishing the machinery of institutional segregation.* (Whittaker, 1991.)

The Centre for Studies on Integration in Education – campaigning for change

> *We see the ending of segregation in education as a human rights issue which belongs within equal opportunities policies.* (Centre for Studies on Integration in Education, 1990.)

The Centre for Studies on Integration in Education (CSIE) is a nation-wide UK organisation which promotes good practice in integration. Useful information can be drawn from their literature, some of which has implications for adult and further education and for the community in general.

Mark Vaughan has written about the effect of segregated education in creating the prejudices that are faced by adults with learning difficulties:

> *Integration in education . . . is about trying to create a fairer and more inclusive society. The most important message to put across today is that continued segregated education contributes to discrimination, misunderstanding and prejudices experienced by adults with learning difficulties.* (Vaughan, 1990.)

Vaughan argues that integration offers benefits to all, in that the process 'represents a long-term enrichment of the quality of life for all, whatever their abilities or disabilities' (Vaughan, 1990).

CSIE sees integrated education from school and into adulthood as fundamental to the achievement of full citizens' rights for people with learning difficulties or other disabilities. At the same time it also raises awareness for other people in the community:

> *Support for the principle of integration in education rests on the rights of people with disabilities or difficulties in learning to the same opportunities for self fulfilment as other people. These opportunities should arise in the community if barriers of ignorance, fear and prejudice are to be broken down, barriers which ultimately lead to discrimination and a refusal to accept all people as full members of society.* (Centre for Studies on Integration in Education, 1989.)

The Integration Charter (Centre for Studies on Integration in Education, 1990) points out that for Care in the Community schemes to work effectively, people in the community need to extend friendship and acceptance to people with learning difficulties or other disabilities. Integrated learning can foster an understanding that difference can be valued and not shunned.

CSIE has some useful ideas about what integration is and is not, which are pertinent for adult and further education staff.

- Integration is not about making people with learning difficulties or other disabilities 'fit into' the system.
  Integration is about institutions themselves changing and adapting.
- Integration is not 'about minimising diverse needs'.
  It is about accepting diversity, and valuing individuals as people first.
- Integration is not 'about the end of special education'.
  It is about the transfer of the 'best practice' in special education to mainstream settings (Vaughan, 1990).

Vaughan has observed that CSIE staff are often asked if integration is a good idea, which is 'like asking is Tuesday a good idea? But just as there are good and bad Tuesdays, so there is good and bad integration' (Vaughan, 1990).

Developing the quality of social integration

Integration *can* go wrong. Helene Richards, reporting on the MENCAP Leisure Integration Project, has described what happened when a new volunteer stepped in to work with a student with learning difficulties in a woodwork class:

> *The volunteer made some valuable observations. David was totally isolated in the class. No-one spoke to him or took an interest in his project. At coffee time, he went to the canteen but the other students brought their snacks and stayed in the classroom.* (Richards, 1991.)

Whereas the previous volunteer had concentrated on helping David to make well-finished pieces of furniture, the new volunteer's concern was primarily 'to help the class accept and include David in their group'. The quality of social integration is part of the overall experience.

In Canada and America, the concept of 'circles of support' is used to support people with learning difficulties or other disabilities in integrated settings. Fellow students are asked to take an active responsibility for welcoming and supporting an individual with a disability. Circles of support to enable adults with learning difficulties to be a part of the wider community are being developed in one or two places in Britain. The ideas of Canadian and American inclusive educators were disseminated in Britain by means of international conferences held in England and Wales in 1991 and 1992. Marsha Forrest and Jack Pearpoint, both from Toronto, explained at British conferences in 1991 that their one criterion for inclusion was that 'the person had to be breathing'. Making Action Plans (MAPS) is a development in which circles of support members meet to dream a future with and for a person with learning difficulties, and to contrast this with a nightmare vision. In this way, new opportunities can be created and worst scenarios avoided.

Moving towards integration

The climate is gradually changing, as people realise that adults with learning difficulties have the right to the full curriculum range, delivered in the same context as that for other learners. The model is starting to move from segregated groups and a limited curriculum towards integrated learning and access to wider learning opportunities. This has clear implications for staff development. The responsibility for all staff has been defined:

> *Integration challenges the notion that students with special needs require the expertise of specialist teachers and institutions whose boundaries are well defined, but implies extending the knowledge and skills of all teachers, thus enabling them to respond appropriately to individual need. (DES/HMI, 1987.)*

Developments require a shift of attitudes, approach and resourcing. The next chapter addresses some of the barriers that get in the way, and suggests some possible solutions.

What do you think?

All or nothing?

It is the view of some people that offering integrated learning is the only valid and valuable form of education for adults with learning difficulties who have made informed decisions about their learning.

A range of provision?

Others argue that a continuum of provision should be available, both discrete and integrated, so that students can choose their preferred option. An important DES report describes how colleges can adapt to provide:

> *a flexible range of provision . . . incorporating an array of possibilities and an opportunity for progression, not just a simple choice between mainstream and special courses.* (DES/HMI, 1987.)

A case for separate groups?

There is an argument for retaining a degree of separate provision for adults with learning difficulties. The common experiences of adults with learning difficulties often form the focus for self advocacy courses and groups. Much in the same way that other oppressed groups (such as people from black and other ethnic minority groups or women) have argued for space for themselves, shouldn't there also be time and space for people with learning difficulties to meet together? Success in discrete classes often provides evidence to parents and carers that integrating adults with learning difficulties in colleges and adult education centres can work.

Is integration what students want?

What do people with learning difficulties themselves want from the learning situation? Some people have clear ideas, as in the self advocacy group which complained to the local college that they were always put in separate classes for people with special needs.

Does integration have backing from managers and planners?
Do they think that integration should be developed?
   Are they aware of the issues and resource implications?

Is integration what staff and parents or carers want?
Willingness and co-operation are needed to make integration work.
   Are people motivated to make the effort?

Are the resources there?
Co-ordinating and monitoring integration takes time. Can your organisation allocate or re-direct time and resources to make things happen?

What do we mean by integration?
The Warnock Report (DES, 1978) has made distinctions between **social integration** (shared socialising), **locational integration** (sharing places) and **functional integration** (sharing activities). How do these types of integration work in practice in your setting?

What about numbers?
Many integration schemes restrict numbers of people with learning difficulties in a group to two. Is there an ideal number? Experience suggests not, and that flexibility is required.

What about quality?
How can the quality of the integrated experience be evaluated for all parties concerned?

Think for yourself

What are your views on the integration debate?

Talk to three or four other people (maybe a colleague, a student, a parent or carer, and a manager) and find out what their views are.

References

Centre for Studies on Integration in Education, 1989, *Integration: The main arguments. A Factsheet.*

Centre for Studies on Integration in Education, 1990, *The Integration Charter.*

DES, 1978, *Special Educational Needs. Report of the Committee of Enquiry into the Education of Handicapped Children and Young People (The Warnock Report).* London, HMSO.

DES/HMI, 1987, *A 'Special' Professionalism.* London, HMSO.

DES/HMI, 1989, *Students with Special Needs in Further Education.* Education Observed, 9.

Forrest, L., 1991, 'Exclusive education'. *Passport*, Autumn, 2.

Richards, H., 1991, 'Leisure opportunities for adults with learning disabilities'. *Report of the MENCAP Leisure Integration Project.* MENCAP, London Division.

Vaughan, M., 1990, 'Focus on CSIE'. *Contact*, Summer. RADAR.

Whittaker, J., 1991, 'Segregation still rules on the college campus'. *Community Living*, January.

Chapter 2

Barriers to Integration

Numerous barriers can obstruct the development of integration. John O'Brien from Georgia, USA, speaking at an inclusive education conference in Britain, described these as the 'monsters' that bar the way to full inclusion. Joe Whittaker has reported on O'Brien's presentation: 'Just when we think we have overcome one barrier – fear, for example – a new unforeseen one, such as complacency, emerges to hinder progress. John [O'Brien]'s story-line highlighted the need for continual vigilance against obstructions to full inclusion, to see inclusion as a philosophy of life and not simply the placement of a person from a devalued context into a valued community' (Whittaker, 1991).

> *Barriers to integration are not thrown up by the nature or the*
> *severity of an individual disability or difficulty in learning,*
> *but by prejudice.* (Centre for Studies on Integration in
> Education, 1989.)

This section identifies some commonly reported blocks and
barriers to integration and highlights some possible ways of
overcoming them.

Safety in familiarity: attitudes of special educational needs tutors

Provision in segregated groups which, as one parent put it to me,
'lumps people together by virtue of their disability', has sometimes
operated in the same way for years. These segregated groups can
become safe territory for some lecturers in special educational
needs, who fear that other lecturers will not understand their
students. They see mainstream groups as a risk to their students,
who have to be prepared for integration. A number of places run
pre-integration courses. Who decides when someone is ready to
join in with other people?

Barrier
It is easier to run the same old groups.

'Anyway, the tutors and students like it that way!'

Step forward
Staff development sessions in order to help special educational
needs tutors recognise the value of integration.

Fear or lack of co-operation: attitudes of general tutors

Some general tutors are described by colleagues as being 'very
fearful' of working with adults with learning difficulties.

Barrier
As one co-ordinator said: 'The lack of co-operation of colleagues is the biggest barrier.'

Step forward
Staff development sessions for all tutors on working with adults with learning difficulties.

Concern from parents and carers

While some parents, relatives and carers wholeheartedly support the concept of integrated learning, for others it can be seen as a risk to their adult son or daughter, from which they need to be protected.

Barrier
'I was worried to see Emma going off with normal people!'

Step forward
Other parents are often willing to advocate the benefits of integrated learning. In some cases, parents or relatives have enrolled as co-students.

Parents and carers as diffident learners

Some parents or carers may lack confidence in their abilities as learners. They may also have had unsatisfying educational experiences which colour their view of other people's learning.

Barrier
'I don't know what he/she wants to do painting for. It'll only make a mess.'

Step forward
Offer opportunities for parents and carers to experience learning in their own right (perhaps through taster sessions) to give them a positive personal experience.

Safety in numbers

Enrolling a group of students with learning difficulties in a special department is relatively straightforward at a college of further education. Enrolling individuals with learning difficulties across departments is more complex, particularly where support is coming from a learning support department. Who counts the student hours or the tutor hours? To whom do the students, their tutors, and their fees 'belong'?

Barrier
'It is fiddly to organise.'
'We haven't got the time to sort it out!'
'And it would affect our enrolments.'

Step forward
Integration takes time to arrange, and this should be recognised in terms of staff timetabling and remission from teaching. A few places now have full-time integration development workers, and the impact of these roles has been substantial.

Expenses for fees and course materials

Students with learning difficulties are often on limited incomes, and some courses are expensive in terms of fees and materials.

Barrier
'They couldn't afford it anyway.'

Step forward
Voucher schemes and concessionary schemes such as Coventry's Passport to Leisure and Learning can include students with learning difficulties. Some concessionary schemes give a 75 per cent discount to unwaged people or those on benefits, with a full waiver for hardship. In other cases, funds have been provided to give individual help with fees and materials.

Student support

Students with learning difficulties may need additional support in the classroom in order to get the most out of the learning situation.

Barrier
'She could never manage on her own.'

Step forward
Various schemes offer support by drawing in people to support individuals with learning difficulties, such as:

- a co-tutor to support the tutor in charge
- a teaching assistant
- a co-student, recruited from the existing class
- a volunteer, recruited specifically to support a student with learning difficulties
- group-home or day-centre staff
- friends
- relatives.

Tutor support

Tutors new to working with adults with learning difficulties may feel anxious about their roles and responsibilities. Myths and stereotypes may need dispelling.

Barrier
'Of course, I've never done this sort of thing before.'

Step forward
An induction session or course with practical experience followed up by ongoing support can be effective in convincing tutors that

teaching adults with learning difficulties is about good practice in teaching and learning, rather than a mystical skill.

The general public

Some people harbour visions of the general public making a mass exodus when people with learning difficulties enrol as students.

Barrier
'The other students wouldn't like it, you know. We can't risk losing or upsetting our clientele. People vote with their feet and we have to be realistic.'

Step forward
Research and evidence shows that people don't leave classes because adults with learning difficulties are present. In the rare cases where negative reactions occur, it may be that the integration has been badly handled. An equal opportunities philosophy and statement helps to make students aware of the policy behind integrated learning. Managers, governors, and staff may need disability equality training to consider their own attitudes.

Transport

It is much easier to transport a group of ten students with learning difficulties in a minibus than to arrange for the ten students to get to college at different times for different classes.

Barrier
'Even if we arranged everything else, the students still couldn't get there!'

Step forward
Solutions employed have included:

● teaching students to travel independently

- resourcing transport by paying for taxi fares
- using volunteers to provide transport
- approaching local bus companies to provide tailored bus routes
- using services such as Community Transport or Dial-A-Ride.

Losing money

Students with learning difficulties are usually given a favourable weighting of resources (for example, one and a half, two or three times the usual quota) under the Schemes of Delegation applied to further education colleges. However, in a number of places, the weighting only applies to discrete, segregated groups. The extra resource allocation is lost when people with learning difficulties join ordinary classes. Similarly, in adult education, people on low incomes who have their fees waived, including adults with learning difficulties, 'don't count as people' on registers, as one interviewee put it.

Barrier
'There's no financial incentive to integrate.'

Step forward
Sheffield LEA gives an integration premium to colleges in order to develop integrated learning. Other places ensure that students with learning difficulties and volunteer co-students have fees met so that they 'count' on the register. One area assesses the weighting by keeping a support register and uses the money for support tutors.

When classes do not run

Most adult education classes need a minimum number of students to be viable. Thus, classes which are advertised do not always recruit enough people and have to be cancelled. This can lead to disappointment for prospective students with learning difficulties who have made their choices.

Barrier
'There is no guarantee that advertised adult education classes will actually run.'

Step forward
The need for a viable student number is an issue which affects all adult learners. Some schemes cover this scenario by asking adults with learning difficulties to make back-up choices in case their first choice of group does not run.

What to integrate into?

Opening up the curriculum poses complexities – whether to approach tutors with known sympathetic and positive attitudes, or whether to go for subject choices which could be 'high level' and certificated.

Barrier
'What classes would be "suitable"?'

Step forward
Handing responsibility for decision-making to students where possible, and in so doing avoid the policing of subject options by staff. At one college, students with learning difficulties have joined certificated options and participate at their own pace and level.

Students with little or no speech

Working with students with learning difficulties who have little or no speech presents a particular challenge.

Barrier
'How can we include them if we don't know what they want?'

Step forward
Orchard Hill FE Centre in Sutton gives students with profound and complex learning difficulties direct experiences of subjects such as cookery and pottery, and then asks them to indicate their choice of option by pointing or looking at a choice of physical objects – for instance, a mixing bowl and spoon, or a lump of clay.

Isolation

A sense of isolation is often experienced by individuals working to develop integration.

Barrier
'I feel so isolated in what I'm trying to do. Am I the only one?'

Step forward
Building up a team to develop integration is one solution. Networking with other people doing similar work in your region can also offer support. Staff working in health authorities, social services departments or voluntary organisations are likely to share similar objectives with education tutors working towards integration. Are there ways in which you could work more closely together? Can you obtain management support for joint approaches?

Think for yourself

What emphasis does segregated, discrete provision have in your local area?

What opportunities currently exist for adults with learning difficulties to experience integrated learning? What could be developed, and who would need to be involved?

What staff development is needed to promote inclusive education? Who would provide it, and how would it be resourced?

How are parents and carers informed of developments in integrated learning?

Do enrolment procedures, student hours and resource allocation systems support or block integration?

Is there a system for remission of fees and course expenses for adults with learning difficulties?

Has disability equality training been provided for senior managers and governors?

What system exists or could be developed for transport and transport training to enable adults with learning difficulties to travel to individual classes of their own choice?

Who chooses which integrated classes adults with learning difficulties join, and who determines and costs the level of support required?

Is there a budget to meet the costs of support staff or the co-ordination and maintenance of a volunteer scheme?

References

Centre for Studies on Integration in Education, 1989, *Integration: The main arguments. A Factsheet.*

Whittaker, J., 1991, 'Challenging segregated services'. *Community Living*, July.

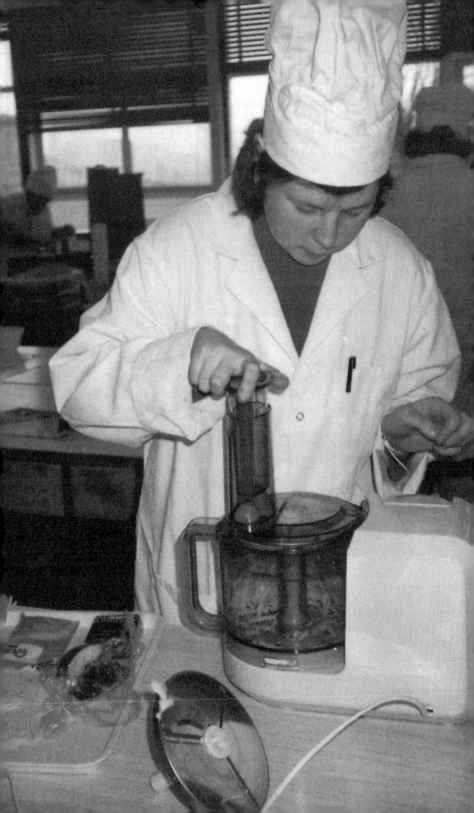

Chapter 3

College Approaches

Colleges around the country are developing different methods of integrating adults with learning difficulties. This section illustrates in brief the approaches taken by five different colleges in opening up access to the curriculum for adults with learning difficulties.

Some people see things as they are, and ask 'Why?' Others dream about how they might be, and ask 'Why not?'

Bournville College: building a culture of support within a whole college approach

Patricia Twyman, Principal of Bournville College in Birmingham, considers that the move 'from idealism to action' at her college has been supported by:

- a very good relationship between the college and the local education authority
- a highly supportive governing body which includes two industrial governors in wheelchairs
- a sympathetic college senior management team, of whom the Vice Principal, a Director and an Assistant Director have a track record of work with adults with disabilities or learning difficulties; another Assistant Director is a specialist in Adult Education and Adult Basic Education (ABE)
- substantial funds earmarked for developments in special educational needs, from various departments of the local authority, such as the City Engineers' Department
- a clearly stated equal opportunities policy and code of practice.

The aim is to work towards functional integration. Physical access is seen as being of paramount importance:

Physical access has always been a priority. Unless you tackle that one successfully, you will never achieve full curricular access. (Patricia Twyman.)

The college was not built with learning support in mind; yet with adaptations and alterations, only three of the college's 17 areas remain difficult to access. Staff development across the board is an important part of the process in building a culture of support, and staff commitment at all levels is expected. A Learning Support Unit, which ranks equally with the college's other 15 units, currently supports students with learning difficulties and other disabilities. In the future, it is possible that the unit could be dispersed, with staff working across the college. A recent development has been to establish a strong network of representatives, one from each of the other 15 units, to work closely with the Learning Support Unit.

There is a long tradition of learning support work at Bournville College; this area of work began in the 1960s. Of the college's total annual enrolment of 7,000 students, approximately 250 have learning difficulties or other disabilities and require learning support. The Learning Support Unit has almost 20 staff with different specialisms, while in addition a number of staff in other units have qualifications in special education. Bournville College's Mission Statement refers to the college's social agenda, which includes offering provision for people with disabilities. This statement is reproduced in the college prospectus, which also incorporates photographs of students with disabilities. Patricia Twyman describes this as part of the 'front-of-house' image given to the Learning Support Unit, which is also located centrally in the college. Bournville College has a policy of assisting other local education authorities and colleges to promote learning support, and has been able to offer advice to a number of authorities in England, Wales and Northern Ireland.

At Bournville College, staff development and access to the curriculum is linked to institutional change and development, with a strong management team supporting change.

Gateshead College: learning support across the curriculum

Gateshead College has recently opened up full access to the curriculum for adults with learning difficulties. Students can choose programmes of study in any area of the college, and receive individual support to make their participation as full as possible.

GATESHEAD COLLEGE
LEARNING SUPPORT ACROSS THE CURRICULUM

SUPPORT PRIOR TO ENROLMENT & EXIT

Information
Guidance
Admissions
APL
Assessment Testing
School Liaison
Community Outreach
Careers Education
Access Development

SUPPORT THROUGH LEARNING RESOURCES

Flexible Learning Environments
Flexible Delivery

- Language Support
- Basic Skills Support

LEARNING SUPPORT WITHIN A PROGRAMME OF STUDY

Comes from – Structure of
- Learning Experiences
- Assessment Methods
- Team Operation
- Tutorial Input
- Resourcing
- Evaluation & Review

Personal Counselling
One-to-one Support in Classroom and Other Environments
Personal Care
Finance

ADDITIONAL SPECIALIST SUPPORT AVAILABLE TO ALL

Reviewing
Recording
Action Planning
Personal Development
Careers Education – Progression
Health Education

SUPPORT THROUGH THE TUTORIAL SYSTEM

The Partners in Learning Scheme enables adults with learning difficulties to study with the support of a volunteer partner who is unemployed. Both partners work towards taking a recognised qualification (such as the City and Guilds 333 Cookery certificate) or join in with non-vocational classes such as art or photography. In the future it is hoped to obtain backing from the local Training and Enterprise Council for the volunteer partners to gain elements of the NVQ 926 Trainers' Award.

An outline of how learning support is organised across the college is shown on page 34.

Langley College: a full-time pastoral support role

Jenny Murphy co-ordinates integrated learning for adults with learning difficulties and other disabilities at Langley College. Students choose the courses they would like to do, and Jenny liaises with tutors and offers support to both students and tutors. The role is one of support and co-ordination with a strong pastoral element. Students with learning difficulties have chosen widely, and have joined in with courses ranging from outdoor pursuits to City and Guilds courses. Although Jenny is prepared to work in the classroom alongside tutors and individual students, this has not in fact been required. Some of the tutors describe 'forgetting' that some of their students are labelled as having learning difficulties. This is a measure of how comfortable they feel with the scheme, which has been enormously successful.

About 15 individuals with learning difficulties have selected and studied the following courses:

- interior design
- textiles
- sewing
- pottery
- brickwork
- watercolour painting
- beauty
- woodwork
- outward bound activities such as canoeing and rock climbing
- painting and decorating
- hairdressing.

Painting and decorating is a vocational City and Guilds course, which is being studied by a young man with severe learning difficulties. He attends college for a long day (9 a.m. to 8 p.m.) in order to do this. It is hoped that he will get a City and Guilds qualification for his practical work. He also joins in with the theory classes, and shows that he is absorbing some of the information. Two of the students with learning difficulties are deaf, and are accompanied by support signers provided by the social services department, who are supportive of such integrated learning opportunities and meet the fees. There are no 'special needs tutors' as such; instead tutors are provided with support by Jenny Murphy if this is required. Both tutors and students have grown in confidence.

> *The college as a whole is supportive. Tutors bend over backwards to be accommodating. The majority of staff are keen and helpful.* (Jenny Murphy.)

Access to provision is facilitated by by-passing the usual enrolment procedures, as students with learning difficulties can have additional time to complete the admissions forms at home or at their centres. Once at college, students are treated 'just like other students'.

Wrexham College: support in the classroom and access to a Nursery Nurses' course

At NEWI in Wrexham, adults with learning difficulties select courses across departments. A full-time lecturer and two part-time staff then support individual students in the integrated settings. The support staff have to develop skills in a wide variety of subjects – from typing to bricklaying – in order to work with the students, who have severe learning difficulties.

When a number of adults with learning difficulties expressed an interest in childcare, links were explored with the nursery nurses' department. This fruitful liaison has led to four students with learning difficulties learning alongside nursery nurse students for a module on play. The National Nursery Education Board (NNEB) has agreed to validate a Foundation Skills in Childcare certificate in play skills for the participating students. The college staff hope that, given a modified curriculum and an extended period of study, the students with learning difficulties will also be considered for the full NNEB qualification.

The inclusion of students with learning difficulties on vocational courses has been extended to the catering department, where students are given the opportunity to do a modified and extended course to enable them to obtain a qualification, working alongside other catering students. The funding for this initiative has come from the All-Wales Strategy, with the college contributing a number of tutor hours to supplement the full-time post.

Difficulties have arisen from college re-organisation and from key staff moving on. Joy Verrier, who has been closely involved with the scheme as a teacher based with the community team for people with learning difficulties, comments that: 'It has been a testing time, with trial and error. It takes time to make links across departments – you can't do it overnight.' Joy sees clearly the value of the inclusive policy, and observes that 'It's about the acceptance of human rights.'

Chippenham College

When Chris Sumter came into a new post at Chippenham College, she was offered a base at an annexe some distance from the main site. In the interests of an inclusive approach, she requested space in the main building. Chris co-ordinates full-time provision for young adults with severe learning difficulties. She initially approached staff to see who would be willing to take one or two students with severe learning difficulties in their groups. Since the original approach, other tutors have come forward. Where needed, support in the classroom can be provided by Chris or by a non-teaching assistant. Students with learning difficulties have elected to join the following courses:

- first aid
- GCSE car workshop
- GCSE art
- City and Guilds catering
- equestrian studies
- needlecraft
- caring

- French
- Cambridge modular computing
- sports studies
- photography
- horticulture
- hairdressing.

Six students with learning difficulties have now taken and passed their test on Emergency First Aid, and were awarded certificates by the Principal.

The students with learning difficulties have made good social links and mix in with other students in the refectory. Ventures such as a car wash scheme have helped the students with learning difficulties to gain confidence around the college. Chris Sumter offers individual tutorial support, and backs up the integrated programmes with separate options on self advocacy and sex education. Some of the students have elected to do work experience according to their personal interests, which have included work at a riding stables, a nursery school and a canteen.

An annual residential week pairs students with and without learning difficulties to work together. This is a learning experience for both groups, who last year went to the River Dart Outdoor Pursuits Centre. Canoeing, rock climbing, camping, an assault course, a parachute jump, caving and riding were some of the activities on offer.

Chris Sumter says that choices open to all students on Wednesday afternoons are being selected by the students with learning difficulties:

> *Students on the course now operate their right to join in the activities available on a Wednesday afternoon in the options programme. Activities followed by the students include needlecraft, welding, hairdressing, Tai-kwon-do, trampolining, photography, sport at the leisure centre. Most of these are now unsupported, or mainstream college students partner the students with learning difficulties to support them. The students have*

developed their independence skills, and now operate their right to free choice quite strongly.

Think for yourself

What options for integrated learning exist at your local college?

Does integrated learning have the support of senior managers?

How could access to wider opportunities be developed?

What support structures would be needed?

What would the resource implications be?

Chapter 4

The Linking Scheme

Inter-agency co-operation in Dorset

A number of areas have developed success-ful integration into adult education schemes. Dorset's Linking Scheme has been established by close collaboration between the adult education service, the social services department and by local MENCAP societies, all of which contribute to financing the initiative. Currently operational in Bournemouth, Poole and Christchurch, the Linking Scheme is now hoping to expand to the rural areas of the county.

> *It's a good experience – to get out of the house, learn new things and meet new people. I'm learning to cut out patchwork and sew it up.* (Elizabeth, Linking Scheme student.)

The Linking Scheme enables adults with learning difficulties to take part in adult education classes in the Bournemouth, Poole and Christchurch conurbation. It is an interesting example of the way in which different agencies have worked closely together in order to provide the ideas, impetus and resources needed to get the scheme up and running.

The original idea grew from a piece of work by a Certificate in Social Services student at one of the local day centres, who had made a study of the Hampshire New Ways integration into adult education scheme. This study sparked off discussions in 1988 between interested individuals from MENCAP, adult education and social services departments. A project proposal stemmed from this, and in 1989 the first part-time project co-ordinator took up post. Due to the scheme's success, a second part-time project co-ordinator was appointed in April 1991.

How the scheme works

Students with learning difficulties are matched with volunteer co-students who share similar learning interests. In the autumn term of 1991, 50 students with learning difficulties were paired with 50 volunteer co-students. The cost of fees and travel for volunteers is met by a budget jointly funded by the education and social services departments, which also pays for the salaries and travel of the two project co-ordinators. Local MENCAP societies welcome applications from individual students with learning difficulties in order to pay for course fees and/or materials, which can be expensive for subjects like cookery and photography. Students with learning difficulties are currently joining in with a wide variety of adult education classes, which include badminton, beginners' guitar and Hebrew. An inter-agency management committee oversees the work of the Linking Scheme.

The parents' perspective

Through local MENCAP societies, parents have been actively involved in providing support for the scheme by helping to set it up and by financing fees and materials for students with learning difficulties. They are also prepared to step in and substitute for a volunteer in an emergency, so that the student with learning difficulties does not miss out. Offers of help in recruiting volunteers at enrolment time and on taster days have also been valuable. Les Hickman of Bournemouth MENCAP outlines the strengths of the scheme and says:

> *It's fantastic! All people with learning difficulties should have this opportunity. It's a basic human right.*

She sees the advantages for all parties involved, and has thought carefully and clearly about the issues as follows:

The person with a learning difficulty can:

- enjoy a leisure activity of their choice
- join in with a 'normal' activity
- meet ordinary people in an ordinary setting (not a disabled setting)
- overcome low self-esteem and gain confidence
- be treated as an adult
- have a co-student who works alongside them
- build relationships with people other than professional workers
- gain confidence to go on their own to an adult education class.

For the befriender/co-student, the scheme:

- enables them to go to a class of their choice and also help a person with learning difficulties
- enables them to understand more about learning difficulties and to get to know the disabled person as an individual – not as a handicapped person
- offers support meetings – volunteers know they have professional support for any queries or problems
- enables them to gain an insight into coping with disability within family life
- gives them the chance to see a disabled person as an individual
- changes attitudes and enables them to talk to others positively.

For the tutors, the scheme:

- enables them to see a person with learning difficulties as a member of the class
- changes attitudes and dispels such negative ideas and myths as people with learning difficulties are 'violent' and 'not clever enough for my class'
- provides support, as they know the befriender is responsible and they also know it is part of a scheme with professional support and organisation
- enables tutors to feel proud of their achievement and spread the word of the scheme's success
- prompts thoughts about access to buildings.

Other students in the class:

- can get to know a person as an individual – not as a 'handicapped person'
- can see the positive side of people with learning difficulties.

Parents:

- are encouraged by the fact that their son or daughter is thought able to go to an adult education class
- are reassured by it being a professionally run scheme with volunteer vetting and support
- are enabled to feel that 'someone ordinary' can cope with their son or daughter rather than yet another professional being involved
- can begin to think of their son or daughter as an adult
- are enabled to feel that community activities like adult education classes are also appropriate for their son or daughter
- can appreciate the co-student enjoying the company of their son or daughter.

Towards a development plan for the Linking Scheme

Reaching the rural areas
The scheme currently operates only in Bournemouth, Poole and Christchurch – the most densely populated part of Dorset. The question of how to expand the scheme to the rural areas will be a major part of the scheme becoming a county-wide rather than a localised service. Distance, resourcing, transport, co-ordination and staff support are all factors which require consideration.

Spreading resources and building in progression
As the existing provision is popular and over-subscribed, the co-ordinators, Tracy Carruthers and Judy Parsons, have had to take the difficult decision to allow students a maximum of two years on the Linking Scheme with volunteer co-student support. This factor makes the process of progression an issue – what can students move on to? Will they still require support? Are they able to move on to certificated courses?

Looking at referrals
At present most of the referrals come from social services' day centres. A few people from private homes have joined adult

education classes with the support of the Linking Scheme. Private homes have been asked to contribute £30 per student to join the scheme, in order to balance the social services' funding towards 'their' students. In future it is envisaged that Linking Scheme opportunities will be available for more adults with learning difficulties in liaison with community teams and adult basic education tutors. In liaising with day centres, the onus tends to be on the staff rather than the students themselves to make decisions about who goes on the scheme. In one case, an enterprising day centre user borrowed an application form from a friend and applied in his own right. The placement worked perfectly well. Opening up information and decision-making to students is an area for further development, in order to achieve truly open access. Using pictorial prospectuses in day centres may be a means to develop this approach. A video is also being considered as a means of publicity.

Staff development

Staff development for the two co-ordinators is a difficulty, as few courses, either locally or nationally, address the work that the Linking Scheme does. It can be isolating doing integration work on your own, and Tracy Carruthers and Judy Parsons have found enormous strength in working as a team. They have also appreciated being able to network with colleagues doing similar work across the Hampshire border.

Staff development is also a problem for adult education tutors, as the vast majority are part-timers who are 'hard-to-reach' in terms of training. Tracy and Judy speak to all new tutors as part of the induction programme to explain the Linking Scheme. The individual support which they can offer tutors is also of great value. A newsletter is planned for the Linking Scheme to communicate with all part-time tutors.

Where next?

As part of the moves to develop the Linking Scheme, the following areas will also need addressing:

- Looking at terminology. 'Mental handicap' is still a label used in Dorset.

- Reviewing enrolment procedures. Occasional hiccups have occurred in pre-enrolments, when names have not actually been entered onto registers. The advent of postal enrolments for all students should help to overcome this difficulty.
- Reviewing publicity. The current leaflet is aimed at recruiting volunteers. A more general leaflet could inform parents, carers, other professionals and prospective students about the scheme. A description of the scheme could also be placed in the general adult education prospectuses.
- Planning for expansion to the rural areas. One idea is to have a development day in order that agencies, parents, carers and service users in the rural areas can find out about the Linking Scheme and plan for developments in their areas.

Think for yourself

What opportunities are available in your local area for integration into adult education classes?

Is there a statement welcoming students with learning difficulties and disabilities in adult education publicity and prospectuses?

Is publicity accessible to students with learning difficulties?

What steps would need to be taken to establish an integration scheme?

What resourcing would be necessary?

Which agencies would be interested in supporting and funding an integration into adult education scheme?

What support could local parents' groups, such as MENCAP, provide?

What support would be needed for:

(a) tutors?
(b) students with learning difficulties?
(c) volunteers, if used?
(d) scheme co-ordinators?

How would the issue of fees/numbers on registers be resolved?

What are the key management issues which would need to be addressed?

Who would be responsible for initiating developments and how would they be supported?

Reference

Parsons, G. & Fletcher, H., 1991, *A Right to Learn: A practical guide to positive participation in education for adults with learning difficulties.* NIACE REPLAN (Eastern). [This title is now out-of-print but can be traced through reference libraries.]

Chapter 5

Studylink in Liverpool

A health authority initiative

The Studylink Project has been successful in supporting adults labelled as having profound and multiple learning difficulties or challenging behaviour on ordinary vocational courses in Liverpool, with one-to-one support where needed from inclusive education officers. The work breaks new ground in providing adults with the most severe learning difficulties with the opportunity to participate in mainstream courses. The successful development of the scheme, originally wholly funded by the health authority, has resulted in further funding from other agencies and organisations.

> *'Most people work with the most able students first. We don't.'* (Sheila Cogley, deputy co-ordinator, Studylink.)

The Studylink Project is a three-year pilot project funded by the health authority and based at the Riversdale Centre of the City of Liverpool Community College. It aims to provide new opportunities for adults with learning difficulties who have moved into the community from Olive Mount Hospital, a former children's hospital which catered for people described as having profound and multiple learning difficulties or challenging behaviour.

Studylink enables adults labelled as having profound and multiple learning difficulties to access mainstream vocational courses, with individual support from a team of staff. The philosophy behind the scheme is stated in the Studylink leaflet:

> *We believe that the entire range of college facilities should be available to everyone regardless of the extent of their disabilities. Traditionally people with disabilities have been denied access to mainstream further education provision and therefore have failed to benefit from the social and educational opportunities that college life provides for most students.*

The first stage in the process is a 'getting to know you' time, with a view to producing a student profile. An appropriate course or part of a course is then identified, and the Studylink team negotiate participation and then support individual students both in college and work experience placements. Appropriate courses are identified at the 17 sites of Liverpool College by using college publicity and by making use of the local Training and Access Point (TAP). Studylink students currently join in the practical side of vocational courses, and are not enrolled for examinations. Staff would support students in working on theory if appropriate, and it is envisaged that this could happen with future students. Studylink staff visit the site to look at physical access and to discuss the Studylink scheme with staff. If the course and venue are suitable, a Studylink officer joins the course as a participant to analyse the course content. All Studylink staff are experienced in the use of 'Training in Systematic Instruction', which breaks down tasks to be learnt, and also looks at routines, from where people put their coats to the process of going for coffee. Studylink staff also prepare the tutor and the other students for the arrival of the student with learning difficulties. Sometimes physical adaptations, such as the lowering of equipment, have to be planned and implemented. About 50 per cent of Studylink students use wheelchairs.

> *One 25-year-old student was described as ambulant but with a tendency to mutilate herself and others. At Olive Mount Hospital she was frequently sedated or restrained to a chair. She has a tendency to scream loudly. Her first encounter with college lasted less than five minutes due to her screaming. This first, negative experience was overcome, and she now participates in a catering course for two days a week. She spends two sessions a week preparing salads in a wine bar as work experience. She doesn't scream at work – and now only very occasionally at college.*

This student had enrolled on a catering course. Other vocational courses which students have participated in include:

- fashion and design
- horticulture
- screen printing
- manicure and beauty therapy
- photography
- vehicle maintenance
- vehicle spraying
- furniture restoration
- hairdressing
- woodwork.

Tutors have been mostly very helpful, and have found the presence of a Studylink worker highly supportive. Barriers have come down and as one Studylink worker put it: 'When you actually get out there and do it, people aren't as negative as you expect.'

Choice is difficult as the current Studylink students usually have little or no speech and only limited life experiences. Time spent getting to know students is important, as clues to suitable courses can be deduced by careful observation:

Emma loves clothes and is very particular about which colours she is going to wear. Her co-ordination is good. An electronics course was explored, but no physical access was available. Then a half-day Open College course in fashion and design was located, where students work at their own pace. An occupational therapist came in to advise on the correct height for Emma to work at as she uses a wheelchair. An industrial sewing machine was accordingly lowered. Emma has learnt to use the machine, and has made samples like the other students. She has also taught one of the Studylink officers how to thread up the machine. Emma laughed when she got it wrong! Emma's lack of speech is not a barrier to participation – she makes it clear whether she wants to be there or not.

Studylink aims to provide opportunities for students to make friendships with people who are not paid to be with them. Staff work to facilitate this by looking at the culture of a class in terms of age, profile and interests. For example, an older woman interested in her appearance successfully joined a self-presentation class with other women of a similar age. In another example:

Kevin signs but has little speech. He enjoys woodwork, and has joined a carpentry and joinery course which is wheelchair accessible. When he first joined the class, another student pushed his wheelchair in and introduced him to the rest of the class, while the Studylink worker deliberately loitered in the toilets! She did not want to be a barrier between Kevin and the other students. By the time she came in, all of the students were chatting to Kevin and introducing themselves. Kevin mimed that he liked playing the drums and the guitar. One of the students explained that he plays in a band. Kevin has been invited to see the band playing.

Studylink is fortunate in that it is able to work to provide one-to-one support for a relatively small group of students – about 20 students are currently enrolled. As Sheila Cogley explains: 'We'd rather work with a few people and get it right, to prove that it works.' There is sometimes pressure from enthusiastic tutors who say: 'Bring six people and we'll set up a group!', when in fact the strength of Studylink is that it supports individuals in integrated settings. Fees are not an issue in that courses in Liverpool are free to students who are registered disabled or who receive benefits.

Studylink challenges assumptions in that it caters for adults with profound and multiple learning difficulties or challenging behaviour, and integrates them into ordinary vocational courses. The students' support needs and history of institutionalisation make their integration and participation a challenge to the traditional model of segregated, special provision. As Ken Roberts, an Education Officer in Liverpool, asks: 'What are all the other students with learning difficulties doing in segregated cul-de-sacs?'

It is anticipated that the Studylink model will become a blueprint for other areas of the city to learn from, and there are long-term hopes and plans to disinvest in segregated provision and to reinvest in inclusive education.

The Health Authority funds the Studylink programme, which cost £130,000 in its first year of operation. The money was originally going to be used for a day centre in the grounds of a college, where the curriculum would have centred on sensory stimulation and interaction. However, a new health authority director argued that education should be equipping adults for jobs, and not teaching them how to smell or how to taste.

Studylink staff are required to have:

- knowledge of courses available and of options within courses
- contact with course providers, and knowledge of their attitudes towards inclusive learning
- knowledge of physical access
- expertise in course analysis
- expertise in Training in Systematic Instruction.

New developments

As the impact of Studylink spreads, so the project receives new sources of funding. The original team has recently been expanded from six health-funded posts to a team of 13, with backing from various organisations:

- the Merseyside Training and Enterprise Council is funding two posts to support school-leavers from two special schools and to provide vocational training and work experience
- the city's Further Education Development Fund is providing three posts to help students with learning difficulties already attending discrete courses to progress on to vocational training
- Community Integrated Care provides the supported accommodation used by people who have moved out of Olive Mount Hospital. They will be seconding two members of staff to Studylink in order to help students who live in Community Integrated Care houses to join non-vocational courses.

Studylink has been developed to offer an inclusive, integrated and extended range of opportunities for progression into open employment via local supported employment schemes. The Studylink programme is being evaluated by an independent researcher. As Ken Roberts puts it: 'Studylink seriously challenges everything that special needs educators have been doing.'

Think for yourself

What opportunities exist or could be developed for adults with learning difficulties to join vocational courses on an integrated basis?

How can adults with profound and multiple learning difficulties or challenging behaviour be supported to access college courses?

What role does your local health authority currently play?

Is there scope for collaborative work with the health authority?

How could schemes such as Studylink relate to Care in the Community initiatives in your area?

Reference

Information on 'Training in Systematic Instruction' is available from Sarah Woodin, Co-ordinator/Trainer, TSI Ltd. Tel. 0345 282808.

Lowestoft

A social services initiative

The development of integrated learning for adults with learning difficulties at Lowestoft College has been supported by the active involvement of a worker from the social services department. Simon Kent, based at Lowestoft Adult Training Centre, has been able to work full-time to build up links with the college. Support for students with learning difficulties and for college tutors is a vital part of his role.

'For any integration scheme to work, a lot of time and planning needs to go into establishing and developing contacts.'
(Simon Kent.)

Simon Kent is a day care officer employed by Lowestoft Adult
Training Centre. He plays a key role in liaising with Lowestoft
College of Further Education to develop opportunities for adults
with learning difficulties. Simon started this role in a part-time
capacity, but what started as an hour-a-week responsibility grew
into a two and a half day-a-week commitment until, in March
1990, social services managers agreed to commit Simon's job to
developing college links on a full-time basis.

Planning for flexibility

Flexible support for both college staff and students with learning
difficulties has been an essential feature of the work.

*Just as individual students attend different courses to meet their
own needs and wishes, it is necessary to recognise that students
need different levels of support within their classes. For some it
may involve a volunteer working alongside them for the duration
of the course, for another it may mean a degree of support from
me periodically and for others it may only involve an introduction
from me to the tutor. Acknowledging this individual level of
support required by each student hopefully means that he or she
is helped to get as much out of the course as he or she wants
to. Giving different levels of support to students also applies to
the staff teaching them. Each member of staff has different levels
of contact with people with learning difficulties and different
expectations. Consequently different levels of support were given
to them. Again this ranged from me supporting them in class for
as long as required, to weekly meetings, to end of term meetings*

and to visits by the staff to the Adult Training Centre to find out more about the different kinds of programmes students took part in at the centre. Central to my support to staff was that they knew that if they needed support from me, I was available to give it to them. (Kent, 1990.)

Students with learning difficulties have been supported to join integrated classes which include:

- adult basic education
- art for pleasure
- first aid
- French
- dressmaking
- maths workshop
- spinning and weaving
- catering
- nutrition and cooking
- City & Guilds recreation and leisure.

Respecting student choice

The student's individual choice of subject is respected, and one of the first ground rules that Simon negotiated with the college was that students would not be used to fill up vacancies on courses that had already been negotiated.

Suzanne attended a Home Nursing Skills course at college, offered as part of the BTEC First Diploma in Caring course. She said this about the course:

I got on very well with the group. I liked going there because people helped me a lot. I learnt a lot about different things. Different people have different diets. If people are unwell they should have light meals, such as fish, scrambled eggs. We learnt a lot about looking after elderly people, how to wash them and take them to the toilet. We bathed a doll to learn how to bath a real baby. The water must be the right temperature, not too hot and not too cold. I learnt a bit about first aid, how to bandage and how to put a sling on someone's arm. We talked about how to keep things safe at home away from children.

The students with learning difficulties have been able to develop new skills, make new friends and experience fresh opportunities in the context of integrated learning at Lowestoft College. As Simon has commented: 'The benefits are as numerous and as individual as the number of students going to college.'

The range of integrated options available to students has continued to develop over the last two years to meet changing needs. During 1990–1991, a number of students joined different building craft courses such as painting and decorating and brick-work. In conjunction with the community education service, a self advocacy course is now running for adult training centre students and the next course will be opened up to include other people with learning difficulties.

Major developments of existing college options include, for the first time, the interviewing of prospective students wanting to work as kitchen assistants in the college training kitchens. It is hoped that in the future other potential college students from the adult training centre will be interviewed so that the decision on who attends will include college staff as well.

Further developments

Other initiatives have taken place away from the college and the central theme of these has been to offer placements to students in the community wherever and whenever they meet their individual needs. One student now works alongside a volunteer on the Books-on-Wheels service and her work includes helping to restock shelves and cleaning books. Another two students attend a fort-nightly reminiscence group at a local day centre for the elderly. Other placements include working as a volunteer helping to prepare and serve meals at a luncheon club for the elderly.

The emphasis is now on using the college as one of a number of community resources to meet the needs of individuals. The courses at college represent a more formal setting for learning, but other resources in the community, such as voluntary groups, are available to extend the range of informal opportunities in which students can learn and acquire new skills.

Simon's role has developed to involve him in building up a bank of resources so that when a student requests a particular placement, access is available to a wide range of formal, college-based placements, as well as informal, community-based placements to meet the needs of the individual student.

Think for yourself

Can the social services department in your area offer support and/or resources to develop integrated learning?

How can agencies collaborate to further opportunities for integration?

Can secondments of staff across agencies play a role in developing integrated education for adults with learning difficulties?

Reference

Kent, S., 1990, *The Integration of People with Learning Difficulties into Further and Adult Education, Academic Year 1989/1990.* MENCAP.

Chapter 7

Breakaway

Integrated leisure in Leeds

Links between different agencies and the local community have enabled a small-scale leisure integration scheme to develop in one area of Leeds. A community education tutor co-ordinates the linking of adults with learning difficulties with volunteers to follow up individual interests and ideas, in which making choices, trying out new activities and developing friendships are part of the overall learning experience.

> *'I like getting out and going bowling.'*
> *'I like making cakes and going out for a drink.'*
> *'I like going to the pub and playing pool.'*
> *'I like coming here. We do different things and go to different places.*
> *Everyone is nice. I like Alan (the tutor). He says I'm the boss!'* (Comments from participants on the Breakaway scheme.)

Breakaway enables individuals with learning difficulties to access and make choices about leisure, recreation and education. It is a small-scale initiative, which helps up to 12 individuals with learning difficulties to explore the use of their free time with the one-to-one support of volunteers. Students are referred by the local community team for people with learning difficulties. The scheme was established in 1989 by tertiary education, a community team for people with learning difficulties, and by Sharing Care, a voluntary organisation, in association with the church and the local community. All of these groups give ongoing support to the scheme, which is based in the South Headingley/Burley area of Leeds.

The emphasis is clearly on individual choice. Workers on the scheme have witnessed its development:

> *We have moved on from the model of an entire group visiting a sports centre, library, etc. en masse, towards encouraging students to make decisions for themselves about what they would like to do and then to go off, with the help of volunteers, to pursue their own interests.* (Bridget Coates.)

The stated aims of the scheme are:

- to increase personal options and access to social situations
- to enable participants to acquire new skills and make choices
- to enable members to take on new responsibilities for themselves and for others

- to promote personal autonomy
- to increase opportunities for personal learning
- to encourage and support access into wider educational and leisure activities
- to facilitate participation as equals with others in the community.

The Breakaway scheme targets young adults aged between 16 and 30 who tend not to take up other types of provision. On the first Wednesday of each month, participants meet at a church hall to plan the programme of activities for the following three Wednesday nights. This is complex, as co-ordinating who wants to do what and where, with whom, all needs careful planning. A chart has proved useful in logging the activities for individuals, including links with volunteers and transport arrangements. Activities have included:

- bowling
- using sunbeds
- going to the chip shop
- going to the pub or for a pizza
- visiting the cinema or theatre
- walks
- visiting the airport

- going to a football match
- ice skating
- swimming
- badminton
- travelling on a 125 train to Wakefield
- joining a French class at an adult education centre.

The recent installation of a telephone has helped students to take an active role in making their own arrangements.

Working together

The scheme has been made possible by close collaboration between a number of different parties. The church provides free premises and the use of all its facilities (kitchen, games area, games, etc.) for the monthly 'night in', as it is known. Leeds Council pays a tutor, while volunteers have been recruited by Sharing Care, the social services department and the church. Sharing Care also insures the volunteers, and provides some funds. Expenses for volunteers, who are mostly university students and sixth-formers, are met by the scheme. This is important, as activities such as eating out or going to the theatre can be expensive. Volunteers clearly value their participation in the scheme, as the following comments demonstrate:

> *'It's very satisfying to see everyone gaining confidence from going out and experiencing things they've never done before.'*
> *'It's a lively, friendly atmosphere where people are encouraged to discover and enjoy new activities.'*

Difficulties

Timing has been an issue. The social services department envisaged a 52-week-a-year service to begin with; however, the funding allows for term-time provision only. Transport proved a difficulty until Leeds Community Transport were able to provide a bus and driver for those people unable to use public transport.

Another problem has been that as most volunteers are themselves students, there is a sudden dwindling of available volunteers around examination time. Physical access for a prospective student who uses a wheelchair has also presented a challenge. Meeting at a pub with good disabled access has offered a solution to this. Absence for illness or other reasons can throw arrangements for students and volunteers, especially where certain activities (like squash) have to be pre-booked. Fund-raising is an ongoing problem, as volunteer expenses, the phone bill, and transport costs all add up.

Steering group

A steering group meets twice-termly to oversee the scheme. Representatives are involved from tertiary education, the social services department, Sharing Care and from the local community. A student and a volunteer are also important members of this group, whose meetings are also open to everyone attending Breakaway.

Evaluation

Evaluation of individual progress is done informally. However, general observations are positive. Students have grown in confidence, formed friendships and developed the capacity to express wants and to make decisions. They are more able to pursue a social life, and are described as eager to try out new activities and gain fresh experiences.

Think for yourself

What opportunities exist or could be developed for adults with learning difficulties to join in with leisure and recreation activities on an individual basis?

What support or resourcing would be needed to improve opportunities in your local area?

Could the Breakaway scheme provide a model for your area? How can informal networks of support, such as friends and neighbours, be a part of providing valued social opportunities and friendships for adults with learning difficulties?

Can you identify the 'main players' amongst agencies that might be brought together to collaborate in a local scheme in your area?

Reference

Richards, H., 1991, 'Leisure opportunities for adults with learning disabilities'. *Report of the MENCAP Leisure Integration Project.* MENCAP, London Division.

Chapter 8

The NIACE/Lancaster University Summer School

Lancaster University offers an annual and well established summer school for adult learners. A planning team set up by NIACE worked alongside staff from Lancaster University in order to open up the summer school activities to adults with learning difficulties, some of whom came with enablers. Skills and confidence developed as the participants with learning difficulties tackled everything on offer – from archery to poetry readings and lectures on Sartre.

> *'It was a wonderful team spirit.'*
> *'I don't want to go home.'*
> *'I didn't know I could do that.'*
> *'It's like a party every day.'*
> *'I would like to come back.'*

(Remarks from the diary kept by Bevan Gilbert and Lyn Frood.)

In August 1991, adults with learning difficulties and enablers from England and Wales joined in with the Lancaster University Summer School programme for the first time. This week offered all 325 participants the chance to try out new learning activities, to develop skills and to take part in the social programme. People with and without learning difficulties mixed freely in all kinds of settings – from guided walks and rambles to lectures, poetry readings and dances.

Approximately 50 students with learning difficulties joined the summer school, choosing from options which ranged from rock climbing and photography to appliqué and swimming. A number of them had never been away from home before. Fifteen students came unaccompanied, while others had the support of an enabler who came with them. Although the majority of the 25 enablers were staff from group-homes, they also included adult education tutors, a parent, a citizen advocate and a medical student.

Responses from participants

The evaluations asked what students and enablers thought of the NIACE/Lancaster University Summer School. People dictated or taped their responses if they could not write. Comments included the following:

> *'The week has been an unmitigated success.'*
> *'A good idea – impressed with the idea of integration/inclusion.*

Also the variety and flexibility of what was on offer.'
'I liked everything – all the things.'
'I liked birdwatching, archery, British wildlife, Lancaster scenery, food, friends.'

Bevan Gilbert and Lyn Frood kept a diary during the summer school. Here is an extract:

Impressions	**Achievements**
fun	learning new things
laughter	breaking barriers
excitement	more self-awareness
apprehension	satisfaction
confusion	personal growth
co-operation	insight into others'
dedication	problems
courage	friendships.
helpfulness	
sharing.	

Benefits of the week

Roles and labels blurred as adults with learning difficulties, enablers and the 250 other participants on the summer programme learnt, ate and socialised together.

Adults with learning difficulties and their enablers had a chance to try out a wide range of new experiences. Several people have since followed up new-found interests on their return home: for example, one person is now going riding weekly, while others are following up dance and yoga.

There was no selection process and the week offered opportunities for adults with a range of learning difficulties – from moderate and severe through to those people with profound and multiple disabilities.

'It worked well, encouraging a widely mixed ability group to take part. No one was excluded, no matter what their learning or physical difficulties were. This encouraged self-esteem, in that

many of the students were able to help each other.' (Sue Cowan, summer school planner.)

This positive aspect also provided a challenge in terms of access and curriculum.

Confidence developed in a number of ways and is reflected in the actions and comments of the students with learning difficulties:

- Alan decided to join a general games evening. After only one hour's tuition earlier on, he picked up a bow and arrow and hit a near bull's-eye. His efforts easily outstripped those of other participants.
- Theresa discovered the delights of sitting up late drinking coffee in the student kitchen on their accommodation block. Suddenly, realisation dawned as she said: 'Hey! I could invite my friend over here for coffee!'
- Chris realised that he would like to take his interest in fabrics and appliqué further: 'What I'd really like now is to get a grant and do it full time at art college.'

The week was clearly perceived as an important and meaningful experience by those who took part. This is reflected by:

- Lyn and Bevan, who made a beautifully produced and illustrated booklet to record their participation.
- George, who invited people to an event at which he read extracts of his diary from the week, and showed a video recording his achievements.

Planning for support

Considerable preparation went into making the week possible. A planning team of seven experienced and enthusiastic adult educators met to plan the event over a period of 10 months and also worked flat-out during the week. All were fully committed to the principles of an inclusive approach to education. NIACE staff played a key role in co-ordination and liaison, while Lancaster University's willingness to open up the summer school to adults with learning difficulties was an essential ingredient. The Lancaster University Summer School tutors were offered a support meeting, written materials and in-class support where needed. Some were experienced in working with adults with learning difficulties, whereas for others it was a new experience. One of the latter said at the end of the week: 'How can you not like these people? It's impossible!'

What worked well

Keyworker groups
The planning group split the delegates into 'keyworker' groups, so that each had responsibility for making sure that about eight people (a mix of learners and enablers) were settling in, knew their programmes, etc. As one keyworker commented: 'The idea worked well. Relationships were quickly established and students knew who they could go to.'

Flexibility
The planning team were able to be flexible in the type and nature of support offered – and willingly rushed off to support tutors offering subjects as diverse as appliqué, riding and woodcarving. The university summer programme organiser was able to adjust the programme to take on board unexpected demands, as when 25 people expressed an interest in horse riding. As there were only three horses, this proved problematic! Luckily, extra sessions were quickly organised so that everyone could have a turn.

Adapted publicity
Great care and attention was given to producing publicity for the summer school.

- The NIACE application form used large print and a simple format to make it easy to fill in.
- Visual publicity, in the form of posters with large and clear colour photographs, was produced and displayed at Lancaster University in order to help people make choices about what they wanted to do.

- Photos and pictures helped to guide people around the campus.

Taster sessions

The week was designed on the basis that people could try out four learning options on the first two days and then follow up by choosing two of those options to pursue in greater depth on the remaining two days. The concept of taster sessions proved so successful that some students elected to continue 'tasting' for the whole week. As one enabler commented: 'The taster sessions were a good idea, as until Marcus has had a go, he sometimes says no to everything.'

The planning team

The planning team worked fluidly and constructively together to make things work. As one planner observed: 'Each member had their own experience and expertise to bring to the area. Each one of us had a particular specialist area.' Special areas of interest were used by the planning team to offer or arrange for staff development slots for enablers, which ranged from self advocacy to sensory stimulation.

A central base

A central office was kept open as much as possible for people to drop by with queries, and to act as a base for the co-ordination of all activities. Secretarial staff and planners took turns to keep the office staffed. Occasionally students dropped in to share problems and the idea arose of offering a counselling service at a future summer school event.

The challenges

Access and curriculum for people with profound and multiple learning difficulties

The students with profound and multiple learning difficulties found that physical access was a problem for wheelchair users and for those with limited mobility. These students joined in with subjects such as swimming, dance and birdwatching. Putting on additional subjects such as music, aromatherapy and massage would increase options in future summer school programmes. Physical access to social events and to transport for wheelchair users was also a concern as it was limited.

Exhaustion
Time off for enablers, particularly where students with learning difficulties needed constant one-to-one attention, needed to be scheduled in. As this requirement soon became apparent, informal arrangements were made where possible. On a future occasion, this aspect would need a more structured approach, facilitated by more planning group members or volunteer supporters.

The planning group members worked non-stop, supporting and co-ordinating. Because people's enthusiasm knew no bounds, regular breaks were not taken, and so the planners were exhausted at the end of the week. The fact that one or two people who had come independently needed a tremendous and unexpected amount of support was also a drain on staff time and energy.

The days were very full. While some people enjoyed all the activity, others would have preferred to have the timetable 'not so crammed', as one delegate put it. Staff development slots were offered in the hour between the end of the afternoon sessions and dinner – at a time when most people were already tired. One or two students found the programme so tiring that they chose to stay in bed longer towards the end of the week.

Low recruitment from black and other ethnic minority groups
Although applications were encouraged and welcomed from students with learning difficulties from black and other ethnic communities, the recruitment of this section of the community was disappointingly low: approximately four out of the 50 students with learning difficulties. Sessions were offered on black history and Asian culture for those who were interested. One young Asian man had opted in advance to study Asian culture, but then changed his mind nearer the time. 'I know about that already!' was his justifiable feeling.

Cost

The week was expensive to mount. The Baring Foundation and MENCAP City Foundation provided £4,350 towards the cost of the event and individual fees. A charge of £235 per person had to be made to cover all other costs, such as accommodation, meals and tuition. A briefing sheet with the application form provided ideas for obtaining funding for students and enablers. People managed to obtain backing to come from a variety of sources, such as:

- health authorities
- social services departments
- local education authorities
- local firms or businesses
- MENCAP City Foundation or local MENCAP societies
- group-home budgets
- the Prince's Trust.

In addition, some people were able to finance themselves.

Free choice – but an administrative nightmare

It was agreed to let people have total choice of the 20 learning options available on arrival. In principle this worked, in that people could make spontaneous choices then and there after looking at the visual publicity. In practice, organising the wants of 75 people each making four choices of subject proved an administrative nightmare as it had to be organised overnight: literally, as the planners were up until 3.30 a.m. sorting out groups and timing!

Getting lost

The Lancaster University site is large and confusing to find one's way around, especially at first. As one enabler said: 'It was easier to find my way around New York than around here!' Pictorial signs for shops, the swimming pool, kitchens, etc. were helpful in making everybody there more independent. Not everyone, though, had problems:

> *Bryan soon found his way around on his own to the shops and*
> *to the launderette, which he learnt to use – and was always*

surprising his enabler by taking her on different routes and stairwells up to the residential floor.

Mixing in: positive and negative reactions

People with and without learning difficulties ate, socialised and learnt together. There was considerable interest and support from a number of the usual summer school participants, some of whom wanted to find out more about the NIACE scheme.

An evaluation exercise at the end of the week asked summer programme participants the following question:

This week there has been a group of adults with learning difficulties present in the summer programme. How do you feel about their presence?

People were asked to tick one of five responses. Of the 154 responses, the breakdown was as follows:

Very happy: 25% (39 people)
Happy: 32% (49 people)
Neutral: 35% (54 people)
Unhappy: 7% (11 people)
Very unhappy: less than 1% (1 person)

Negative comments on the evaluation forms included the following:

- a warning should have been given that adults with learning difficulties would be present
- the balance of adults with learning difficulties with others was wrong
- courses were affected by the shifting presence of different adults with learning difficulties
- some social events were affected
- some people from caring professions felt that it turned into a 'busman's holiday' for them

- there should have been more helpers in certain situations.

A deliberate decision had been taken not to give other participants advance notice of the NIACE group of learners, on the basis that in the interests of equal opportunities, all adult learners have the right to join in with such events. The only overtly negative reaction during an open meeting came from a nurse working with people with disabilities, who had paid for a holiday to get away from her job. She found herself stepping in to help out, until she made a conscious effort to be detached. It was observed that a large and loud group of American Civil War enthusiasts, dressed in special outfits, probably made as much, if not more, impact on the campus than the students with learning difficulties!

Equally, there were many positive comments. The NIACE group were praised for their exemplary levels of tidiness and cleanliness by the cleaning staff. Other comments included:

> '*An excellent idea . . . it was a pleasure to talk and join in with them.*'
> '*I found it a mind-broadening experience.*'
> '*It has been a good education for me to experience their needs and the things they obviously enjoy.*'

Ideas for another time

A number of practical ideas emerged from the experiences of the week. These included:

- extending pictorial labelling to the minibuses, which take students off campus for activities like rambling and computing
- colour coding bedroom corridors
- re-timing staff development sessions
- extending the curriculum range, especially for adults with profound and multiple learning difficulties
- having a pool of unattached volunteers and enablers to help out as and when necessary

- inviting students with learning difficulties who took part in the summer school to take an active role in planning a future event, drawing on their experiences at Lancaster
- having a map of Britain with people's home areas marked. Many students were away from home for the first time and this would help them to visualise where other people lived.

To conclude, an enabler gives her view of the week:

For me the best part of the week was seeing the changes that occurred to the learners. I found it really gave me energy to see so many people getting so much out of the activities and achieving things they may not have had the opportunity to do except on the course, including being away independently, making new friends and trying out activities they have not previously had access to.

Think for yourself

Do any summer schools or study programmes run in your area?

Do they, or could they, include adults with learning difficulties?

Some areas run segregated summer schools for adults with learning difficulties. How could these be opened up to involve other learners?

Are there other resources in the higher education sector to which adults with learning difficulties might gain access, such as concerts, art exhibitions, sports centres, resource centres?

Reference

Percy, K. & Sutcliffe, J., 1992, 'Integrated summer learning'. *Adults Learning*, January, 127-128.

Gillygate Wholefood Bakery

FINE 'FLOUR
3.5 K.
£1.33p

Chapter 9

Sheffield Education Department

Local education authority support for integration

Sheffield Local Education Authority has provided money to support developments in learning for adults with learning difficulties via an integration premium. Transport to classes has been provided with the co-operation of the local transport company, while a separate budget provides for taxi fares. Norton College is one of the colleges in Sheffield which is working towards expanding integrated opportunities for adults with learning difficulties.

> *'The group is big. I get tired. But I like the videos and the course book.'* (Katy, a student.)

The move towards developing integrated provision in Sheffield's six colleges has come from a tertiary planning group of senior practitioners. Education provision for adults with learning difficulties has been supported by elected members of the Council who have actively sought to protect this area of work as a whole. Social services senior managers were also instrumental in writing a joint report which recommended the increase of integrated provision. The LEA has provided funding and has negotiated for transport to enable adults with learning difficulties and other disabilities to participate in education.

An integration premium – funding incentives

In 1990, Sheffield Local Education Authority set up an 'integration premium' to support the integration of adults with learning difficulties and other disabilities. The integration premium is a fund which provides money for the specific costs incurred in supporting this work. It is part of a large Excepted Item (the Special Educational Needs Fund) in the general colleges' budget, and in 1991/92 the premium stood at £180,000, though there is an intention to increase this amount in 1992/93 if education finances allow this. Councillors on the Education Programme Committee have shown a willingness to protect special educational needs funding from cut-backs, and from the effects of inflation. Special educational needs co-ordinators at the Sheffield colleges make annual bids for money from the fund. The uses have included:

- purchasing care assistant hours to support individual students
- buying-in part-time tutor hours either to support students or to provide cover for full-time staff so that they can support students and staff

- purchasing specialist equipment, aids and adaptations
- improving physical access.

Transport: getting there

Working with the public transport system

If people with learning difficulties and other disabilities cannot get to classes, they cannot participate. The local education officers decided to approach the South Yorkshire Passenger Transport Executive to ask for transport for students with learning difficulties and other disabilities. The Executive agreed to collaborate on the understanding that buses put on would be for fare-paying customers, including members of the general public. Approximately three-quarters of a million pounds was invested by the Transport Executive in a fleet of nine specially adapted buses, painted in the usual colours and fully wheelchair accessible. The routes vary annually to take into consideration the private addresses of students, which are supplied by the special educational needs co-ordinators at Sheffield's colleges.

A fund to pay taxi fares

As the buses only run twice a day – to and from college at the start and end of the day – the service does not meet all individual needs. For this purpose, a separate fund is provided by the LEA to meet individual requests from students with learning difficulties and other disabilities who need taxis to get to and from classes. Dial-A-Ride costs can also be reimbursed from this budget, which in 1991/2 was £30,000.

Steps in the right direction

Moves are being made to break away from segregated provision for adults with learning difficulties in Norton College. The staff are building relationships across departments to provide a base for further integrated provision.

Short courses

Individuals with learning difficulties are, for the first time, being offered the opportunity to choose from a range of learning options which are open to all full-time students on Wednesday afternoons. They have chosen widely from the 10-week blocks available, as the following examples show:

> *Alma has joined the open learning adult basic education group. Students are scattered around a carpeted room in comfortable chairs doing individual work. Alma is doing a piece of writing that relates to her work experience with children in a nursery.*

> *Sharon is in the fitness suite in her tracksuit, surrounded by other young people in leggings and tracksuits – bending, stretching and using the exercise machines to the thud of pop music. Sharon knows a lot about the machines and has been showing other people how to use them. The exercise bikes are her favourite.*

> *Three young women are working in an art workshop – two making and designing ear-rings; a third doing a still life from a basket of fruit and vegetables. Other people in the room are also working on individual projects, such as collage and painting.*

> *Simon and Anna are playing badminton. The sports instructor arranges the session so that they each get a chance to play against the 15 or so other students in the sports hall. Anna has just won a game.*

A college lecturer has been allocated time to pop in informally to see how students with learning difficulties and tutors are getting on. In only its third week at the time of writing, the short course integration is going well. Students with learning difficulties are able to work at their own pace – and with 30 of them joining in individual options alongside 800 other students, the possibilities for blending in and 'losing a label' are real.

GCSE Child Development – a new challenge
Katy, a student with severe learning difficulties but with a reasonable competence in reading and writing, has enrolled on a GCSE Child Development course. She is supported by Karen, a volunteer from Leisure and Recreation Studies, who has a particular interest in working with people with learning difficulties, and who works alongside Katy for a morning of her free time. Karen helps Katy to understand difficult words, such as 'emotions' and 'physical'. She has found that Katy understands the concepts when simple vocabulary is used, and has used pictures to help Katy's recall. Karen also helps Katy with taking notes, as her writing is slow. Katy is particularly looking forward to the child study, when she will observe a young child's development over a period of three months. The tutor is looking at ways of evaluating Katy's participation in the course, and of accrediting Karen's practical experience as a support worker.

Think for yourself

What support and resources can the following give to integrated learning?

- local education authorities
- Further Education Funding Councils
- Training and Enterprise Councils
- councillors
- governing bodies
- health authorities
- social services departments
- voluntary bodies
- charitable trusts.

Does an authority-wide or institution-related policy on integration exist, or is one being developed?

Does a group of senior practitioners advise on resource allocation?

What scope is there for your local authority to negotiate the provision of individualised transport for people with learning difficulties or other disabilities to get to and from classes?

Does a fund like Sheffield's integration premium exist in your area? If not, could such a resource pool be developed?

Chapter 10

Strategies for Change

This section looks at practical steps which have been taken to promote integrated learning in different parts of the country. Messages are also drawn from some of the case studies already presented in the previous chapters.

> *Further education is at a crucial stage and has to recognise that not only the language of special needs has to change but special needs staff have to be seen as facilitators, staff trainers and awareness raisers, demonstrating that special education is about good practice. We have to change the emphasis of the debate in further education away from justifying integration to promoting inclusive education.* (Whittaker, 1991.)

Named contacts and target numbers

An audit of community and further education in Coventry reveals that people are trying to develop integrated learning. They would like to offer more integrated opportunities, but are not sure how to go about it. There is uncertainty about who to contact for help and support.

As a direct consequence of these findings, a network of named contacts will be established to offer guidance and support for integrated learning. This step forward will be backed up in some centres by setting targets for numbers of students learning in an integrated setting. The audit of provision was an inter-agency exercise, with staff from education, health and social services collating learning opportunities across agencies.

Information packs and booklets for support

Some areas are supporting part-time tutors by providing specially prepared development materials.

Greenwich Education Service has produced a staff handbook entitled *We all need support*. Written from the standpoint of teaching adults with learning difficulties or other disabilities, it provides details of the following subjects:

- line managers and specialist staff

- names and interest areas of staff prepared to offer help and advice informally
- resources and equipment available
- telephone helplines
- local information, services and support
- national agencies.

It is a guide to available support and encourages people to make useful contacts: 'Discussing one's work with others is good practice, not a sign of failure.'

The booklet was time-consuming to prepare. Staff time and production costs will be inhibiting factors in updating the handbook, which was compiled by the Integration Project in conjunction with the Special Educational Needs Sub-Committees of both South Greenwich and Thamesside Institutes.

Croydon targeted a number of part-time adult education tutors and provided a resource pack of information leaflets for each tutor. Leaflets from national organisations such as MENCAP and Values Into Action provided information on learning difficulties, alongside leaflets on visual impairment, mental health and other topics. The publicity campaign was backed up by displays and a 'drop-in' stand, which offered advice and information at different adult education centres during the first few weeks of the academic year.

Making a development plan

Dorset (as outlined in Chapter 4) has taken concrete steps to expand its Linking Scheme by embarking on the production of a development plan. It is hoped to expand the scheme to all parts of the county.

Allocating time

North Hertfordshire College found that new links and possibilities for integration across departments were opened up when time was allocated specifically to develop integrated opportunities for school leavers with learning difficulties. The message is that time for liaison needs to be allocated specifically to develop integration rather than expecting it to happen on top of other roles and responsibilities.

Getting support from managers

As outlined in the description of Bournville College in Chapter 3, the support of management is essential. Claire Schimmer, who worked for MENCAP's integration into adult education project in London, says: 'For integration to work, there needs to be solid support for the idea, and that needs to come from the top' (Schimmer, 1988).

Looking critically at the curriculum

Staff in Studylink in Liverpool (see Chapter 5) and at NEWI in Wrexham (see Chapter 3) have identified the importance of an appropriate curriculum. On the Studylink scheme, the practical parts of courses are undertaken. At NEWI, the curriculum has been modified and extended so that students with learning difficulties can learn at a slower pace than other students.

Providing a range of back-up support

Flexible and appropriate support is vital for effective integration. Examples of this include:

- direct support to a tutor and/or a student, which can be 'faded' if appropriate
- tutorial support, as described in Chapter 3, in the sections on Chippenham College and Langley College

- drawing on external support, as in the funding by the social services department for signers for deaf students with learning difficulties at Langley College.

Enlisting the support of parents and carers

The Dorset Linking Scheme shows that parents can be powerful advocates of good practice in integrated learning.

Working with other agencies

As in Sheffield, Liverpool, Dorset and other areas, relationships between agencies can maximise resources and foster new ideas.

Starting small and getting it right

The Breakaway scheme in Leeds is small-scale, but is nevertheless an important initiative (described in Chapter 7). Studylink also works with a small group of students, but believes in developing excellence with a limited number of people as a model for future work.

Dreaming of possibilities

The NIACE/Lancaster University Summer School remained an idea until very recently. As one parent has said: 'When you dream alone, it is only a dream, but when you dream together it is the beginning of reality' (quoted in Thomas, 1991).

Adapting publicity and enrolment processes

Visual publicity and large print were features of the NIACE/ Lancaster University Summer School, while pre-enrolment and enrolment at the student's own pace are features of the work in Dorset and at Langley College.

Setting aside special funds to develop integration

From Sheffield's 'integration premium' through to local MENCAP societies in Dorset funding individual fees and course materials for students with learning difficulties, it is clear that having resources allocated specifically for integration helps provision develop accordingly.

Pairing up: a step in the right direction

Shared learning opportunities have been provided for people with and without learning difficulties in several areas:

- Tameside College ran Absolute Beginners' classes which were open to people with and without learning difficulties
- Skill's regional group in the south-west has organised paired learning events, where tutors and students together try out new subjects
- Elaine Kirk, working in Derbyshire, has run paired cookery, DIY, art and pottery classes, where partners with and without learning difficulties work and learn side-by-side. She has also produced a pictorial questionnaire to survey what subjects adults with learning difficulties would like to learn.

Evaluating the process

Val Williams, tutor organiser at South Bristol College, did a survey of participation in integrated classes. She found that of the 22 students with learning difficulties who joined integrated classes, 12 had been on a preparatory course of taster sessions. The others had joined classes on their own initiative, or had asked to go straight into classes. Social interaction was evaluated in four stages:

being there; *working together*; *personal interaction*; and *friendship*. Most students with learning difficulties worked alongside other students. Where students had developed friendships, it was noted that the classes were especially friendly and informal.

Val Williams next plans to implement a qualitative review to study the experiences and needs for support of students with learning difficulties and other disabilities, to examine the need for further support time and to set up a students' forum to inform future directions of the work.

Evaluation – a student questionnaire

Asking students with learning difficulties who have joined integrated provision to evaluate the course and to make choices for future learning is important. Cardinal Newman Community College in Coventry devised the questionnaire on page 99 to collect information about student responses.

Sharing information

The Northern Council for Further Education produces regular information bulletins entitled *Learning Support – North East*. The bulletins give news of national and regional initiatives, plus contacts and addresses, for practitioners in the region.

References

Greenwich Education Service, 1990, *We All Need Support: A staff handbook*.

Northern Council for Further Education, 1991, 'Partnership.' *Learning Support – North East*. April bulletin.

Northern Council for Further Education, 1991, 'Progression.' *Learning Support – North East*. September bulletin.

Northern Council for Further Education, 1992, 'Participation.' *Learning Support – North East.* May bulletin.

Schimmer, C., 1988, 'A new way – five years on.' In *Innovations in Education for Adults with Special Needs.* SKILL.

Thomas, S., 1991, 'Editorial.' *Passport*, Autumn, 1.

Whittaker, J., 1991, 'Segregation still rules on the college campus'. *Community Living*, January.

STUDENT QUESTIONNAIRE

Student's name: _____

Course: _____

Dear Student

You have been attending a course at Cardinal Newman this term.
Please help us by completing this questionnaire and returning it to
the Community Office by November 29.

1   What did you think of the course?

    a)   I really enjoyed it ☐

    b)   I thought it was alright ☐

    c)   I did not like it ☐

2   Now that you have done this course for a term, do you want to
    enrol for the same course next term?

                Yes ☐   No ☐

3   Do you want to enrol for something different next term?

                Yes ☐   No ☐

4   If you want to enrol for a different course, what other course
    would you like to do?

    Choice 1 _____   Choice 2 _____

    Choice 3 _____   Choice 4 _____

5   Can you tell us what you liked best about your course?

    _____

    _____

6   Can you tell us what you did NOT like about the course?

    _____

    _____

7   Do you want to say anything else? – about yourself? the tutor?
    your helper? the other students? the college?

    _____

    _____

    _____

Thank you for taking the time to fill in this questionnaire.

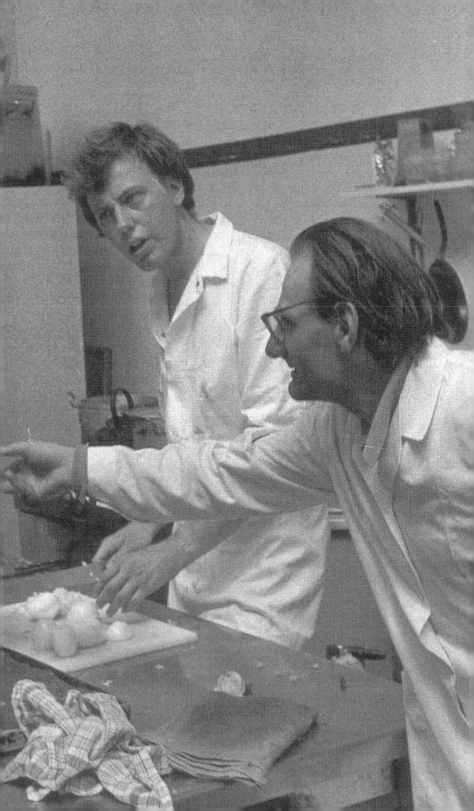

Chapter 11

Checklists for Development and Change

Key areas in the development of integrated learning for adults with learning difficulties are set out in this chapter in the form of questions aimed to help you reflect on the quality of provision in your region. Tick an appropriate box after considering whether the particular aspect of provision is:

1. non-existent
2. under-developed
3. developed
4. well-developed.

Philosophy and policy

	1	2	3	4
Is there a written policy on integrated learning for adults with learning difficulties?	☐	☐	☐	☐
Is the policy set in the broader framework of an equal opportunities code of practice and policy statement?	☐	☐	☐	☐
Is there an action plan set with regard to what is to be achieved, by when and by whom?	☐	☐	☐	☐
Have resources been allocated to implement the action plan?	☐	☐	☐	☐

Gaining support and allies

Have the following groups been targeted for training and/or consultation with regard to the principles and values of integrated education?

	1	2	3	4
Governors	☐	☐	☐	☐
Councillors	☐	☐	☐	☐
Local education authority officers	☐	☐	☐	☐
Senior managers	☐	☐	☐	☐
Special educational needs staff	☐	☐	☐	☐
General education staff	☐	☐	☐	☐
Parent groups	☐	☐	☐	☐
Self advocacy groups	☐	☐	☐	☐
Voluntary organisations	☐	☐	☐	☐
Training and Enterprise Councils	☐	☐	☐	☐
Social services departments	☐	☐	☐	☐
Health authorities	☐	☐	☐	☐
Further Education Funding Councils.	☐	☐	☐	☐

Securing resources

	1	2	3	4
Have resources been allocated to develop integrated learning?	☐	☐	☐	☐

Working with other agencies

	1	2	3	4
What support and resources are available to develop an inter-agency approach to integration? Does policy reflect an inter-agency approach?	☐	☐	☐	☐

Overcoming barriers

Are strategies being developed to overcome the following potential barriers?

	1	2	3	4
● The expense of fees and course materials	☐	☐	☐	☐
● Transport	☐	☐	☐	☐
● Physical access	☐	☐	☐	☐
● Enrolment procedures	☐	☐	☐	☐
● Negative attitudes.	☐	☐	☐	☐

It all takes time

	1	2	3	4
Has adequate staff time been allocated to co-ordinate and support integrated learning?	☐	☐	☐	☐

Supporting staff

	1	2	3	4
Does a staff training programme support general tutors and ancillary staff in working with adults with learning difficulties?	☐	☐	☐	☐

Supporting students

	1	2	3	4
Is flexible support for individual students with learning difficulties available, both in class and around the college or centre?	☐	☐	☐	☐

Publicity

Is information and publicity
available in a large print,
pictorial or photographic format
that can be used by adults with
learning difficulties?

1	2	3	4
□	□	□	□

Do prospectuses and brochures
contain a statement welcoming
students with learning
difficulties and other disabilities?

1	2	3	4
□	□	□	□

Information

Are there opportunities locally
or regionally to set up or
contribute to a newsletter
which can publicise successful
integration activities and offer
case studies of individual
learners?

1	2	3	4
□	□	□	□

Supporting volunteers

Is there a named person to
co-ordinate a volunteer scheme?

1	2	3	4
□	□	□	□

Are resources available, e.g.
for recruitment, training and
transport?

1	2	3	4
□	□	□	□

Is time allocated to support
volunteers?

1	2	3	4
□	□	□	□

Balancing the books

In colleges, does resource
weighting support integrated
learning for adults with learning
difficulties?

1	2	3	4
☐	☐	☐	☐

Defining quality

Is the quality of integrated
learning assessed?

1	2	3	4
☐	☐	☐	☐

Monitoring and evaluating

Are integrated learning
opportunities monitored
and evaluated by all parties
concerned?

1	2	3	4
☐	☐	☐	☐

Where does it all lead?

Is progression built into learning
programmes for adults with
learning difficulties?

1	2	3	4
☐	☐	☐	☐

Are opportunities provided for
education guidance for adults
with learning difficulties?

1	2	3	4
☐	☐	☐	☐

Equal opportunities

Are integrated placements available for individuals from the following groups of adults with learning difficulties?

	1	2	3	4
• Older learners	☐	☐	☐	☐
• Adults from black and other ethnic minority groups	☐	☐	☐	☐
• Adults with profound and multiple learning difficulties	☐	☐	☐	☐
• Adults with challenging behaviour.	☐	☐	☐	☐

Further Reading and Resources

Billis, J., 1984, *A New Way: From theory to practice*, MENCAP.

Care, J., 1986, *A New Way – Five Years On*, MENCAP.

DES, 1989, *Students with Special Needs in Further Education*. Education Observed, 9.

Lloyd, C., 1987, *A Realistic Goal?* Special Needs Occasional Paper 5, FEU/Longman.

MENCAP, 1986, *Integrated Adult Education for People with Learning Difficulties*, MENCAP, London. (A resource p`ck comprising slides, cassette and booklet: only booklets now available.)

Schimmer, C., 1988, 'A New Way – Five Years On.' From *Innovations in Education for Adults with Special Needs*, SKILL.

Sutcliffe, J., 1990, *Adults with Learning Difficulties: Education for choice and empowerment*, Leicester: NIACE/Open University Press.

Values in Action. *Regular Lives*. (A video showing integration in a range of settings in America.)

Willis, P. & Kiernan, C., 1984, *A New Way Evaluated*, MENCAP/Thomas Coram Research Unit.

Journals on Integration

Learning Support – North East. (A bulletin giving information on national and regional initiatives.)
> Available from: Lesley Oates
> Northern Council for Further Education
> Unit 10, Wincomblee Workshops
> White Street
> Walker
> Newcastle upon Tyne NE6 3PJ

Learning Together. (Publishes articles on inclusive education in practice.)
    Available from: Joe Whittaker
    Bolton Institute
    Chadwick Campus
    Chadwick Street
    Bolton BL2 1JW

Passport: Action for Inclusive Living. (Journal of parents campaigning for integrated education.)
    Editor: Sue Thomas
    1 Larkhill Road
    Edgeley
    Stockport

Useful Organisations

Centre for Studies on
Integration in Education (CSIE)
4th Floor
415 Edgware Road
London NW2 6NB
Tel. 081 452 8642

Further Education Unit (FEU)
Spring Gardens
Citadel Place
Tinworth Street
London SE11 5EH
Tel. 071 962 1280

MENCAP
Education, Training and
Employment Department
123 Golden Lane
London EC1Y 0RT
Tel. 071 454 0454

NIACE Rowntree Project
c/o SALP
Charles Street
Luton LU2 0EB
Tel. 0582 22566

Skill: National Bureau for
Students with Disabilities
336 Brixton Road
London SW9 7AA
Tel: 071 274 0565

Training in Systematic Instruction
(Relocating at the time of going
to press.)
Tel. 0345 282808

Values Into Action (VIA)
Oxford House
Derbyshire Street
London E2 6HG
Tel. 071 729 5436

Notes

Notes

Notes